Inspirational Cues

Ex_Turpi

Inspirational Cues
Copyright © 2022 by Ex_Turpi

All rights reserved. No part of this publication may be reproduced, distributed, or transmitted in any form or by any means, including photocopying, recording, or other electronic or mechanical methods, without the prior written permission of the publisher or author, except in the case of brief quotations embodied in critical reviews and certain other noncommercial uses permitted by copyright law.

ISBN: (Paperback)   978-1-953048639
            (eBook)   978-1-639454969

Writers' Branding Revised Date: 10/11/2022

The view expressed in this book are solely those of the author and do not necessarily reflect the views of the publisher, and the publisher hereby disclaims any responsibility for them.

Writers' Branding
1800-608-6550
www.writersbranding.com
orders@writersbranding.com

CONTENTS

PART ONE: PERSEVERANCE

THIS IS MY COUNTRY 3
NOT A STRANGER 4
HER 5
PERSONALITY 7
REALITY 9
RESOLUTION 10
BEYOND TODAY 11
ECSTASY 12
CHANCE MEETING 13
PORTRAIT 14
LEGACY 15
I AM FREE BECAUSE OF YOU 16
CONFESSION 17
SURPRISED 18
MY PLEA 19
GREATEST LOVE 20
ONE MEMORY 21
MY RETURN 22
SO CLOSE 23

PART TWO: HUMILITY

THE IMMIGRANT'S JOURNEY 27
MY FRIEND 28
TRUTH AND CONSEQUENCES 29
A MILITARY SOLILOQUY 30
SUCCESS 31
CONQUER 32
SLEEP 33
WORDS 34

INESTIMABLE 35
PERSPECTIVE 36
THE EFFECT 37
THE TRUE SLF 38
CONSOLATION 39
FAITH 40
FIRST TIME 41
E'GAD! 42
MY PLACE 43
NOSTALGIA 44
SEASONS' END 45
WHEN 46

PART THREE: MORALITY

THE BELL TOLLS 49
I HAD A DREAM LAST NIGHT 50
ON PAR WITH THE OTHER 51
CHRISTMAS 52
HE 53
WHY WORRY? 54
SOLEMN REMINDER 55
EPIPHANY 56
MY PURPOSE 58
GIVING THANKS 59
A ROLE 60
MY JOURNEY 61
CONTRIBUTION 62
GILEAD'S BALM 63
THE INEVITABLE 64
TWO SOON 65
BE STRONG 66
DEATH 68
FRIENDLY ADVICE 69
CHOICE 70

PART FOUR: MORTALITY

I MUST GO HOME AGAIN 73
LIFE'S THOUGHTS 75
MOTHER 76
MY CHOICE 77
MY PRAYER 78
MY VALENTINE 79
NEW YEAR'S 80
SINCERELY 81
NOW 82
INELUDIBLE 83
ON THE ROAD 84
SACRIFICE 85
ON THIS THANKSGIVING DAY 86
PASSING 87
A REASON 88
THIS DAY 89
TIME PASSES 90
TRUTH AND CONSEQUENCES 91
YOUR TASK 92

ABOUT THE AUTHOR 93

Dedicated to the memory of my mother, Gwen, my sister, Carmen who went away from me too soon and to my grandmother, Sarah.

Foreword to *Inspirational Cues,* by Ex_Turpi

Nearly 40 years before his death, Carl Sandburg, the once-hobo become Pulitzer Prize winner and iconic poet wrote thirty-eight definitions of poetry in his work *Good Morning, America.* Two of them came to me like background music and ambient lighting, as I read the poems of Ex_Turpi's *Inspirational Cues.*

> Poetry is the opening and closing of a door,
> leaving those who look through
> to guess about what is seen during a moment
>
> Poetry is a journal of a sea animal living
> on land, wanting to fly the air.

The reading of poetry can never be a passive experience, not if the poetry is successful. It entangles the mind and the soul. For me, there is in the poem that engages an invitation to relate what is read not just to my life but to conjecture about its origins. And so it is not unusual that as I read Ex_Turpi's poems I was driven deeper into the words, as the poems generated not just points of connection with my own experience, but questions and conjectures about the life of the poet. What had occurred, what continues to occur that shaped the soul portrayed in these pages? What is it that crafts a soul at once poignant, wry, realistic and optimistic? In the pages that follow the reader is invited to enter into that question as he or she savors the fruit of that experience and has a new light cast upon his or her own experience.

Annette Sara Cunningham, New York City Autumn 2008

PART ONE

Perseverance

Virgil's Georgics, *Labor Omnia Vincit:*

'Work Conquers All: If we fail, we fail, but screw your courage to the sticking place, and we'll not fail.'

– Shakespaeare's *Macbeth*

THIS IS MY COUNTRY

This is my country; it's like no other
Each one from yon can be my brother
Arrive by land, by sea, by air
Its freedoms, opportunities, treasures to share.

You may be filthy rich or dirt poor
Neither profile will deny you the door
You may enter with nary a skill
Improve your circumstance by dint of sheer will.

The language you speak is of no import
As soon the laws and customs you comport
The caste you claim, the pedigree you bear
Princely or plebian, you can make it here.

You may espouse a deity, or none at all
You may don vestments or discard it all You
may spout your dogma, nay eschew
Agnostic, Atheist, Christian, Muslim, or Jew.

This is my country, perfect it will never be
It is peopled by frail humanity
I assert with all my verve and sinew
For reward of creativity, there's no like venue.

You may be the scion of aristocrats A lowly child of
the proletariat In this land you need not cower
You can rise to the apex of power.

This is my country, thee I'll love for sure 'til for me time is no more
I'll depart this world, grateful that I've been here
Your freedoms, opportunities, treasures to share.

NOT A STRANGER

Cradled in her mother's arms,
Nestled in her stroller
She smiles, buries her head.
Covers her eyes, and smiles again.
She cannot say what she thinks
Yet I understand everything she says.
Her love, her innocence.
Her indiscriminate pleasure at the wave I gave her.
She purses her little fingers;
She waves to me; at me.
She smiles again.
Oh! What ecstasy! What joy!
What beauty! What truth!
Yes, I wish all the world was this pure.

HER

We see her now,
We do not know what she'll be.
We can each safely vow,
She'll be part of me.

Conceived with fealty,
And warmth of our love.
She is born on a day, when
The sun shines brightly above.

We hold her in our arms;
We clasp her at our breasts.
We clothe her with charms;
We kiss her to rest.

She opens her eyes,
She shuts them again.
Her movements and cries:
What pleasant refrain.

She moves from her crib
To the stroller, and then
She crawls on the floor
Reaches at her mother's hem.

She pouts, she smiles
She 'sprinkles,' and more
Our sweet little girl child
Oh! we love and adore.

She goes to the schoolhouse
And lovingly plays.
Her playmates and dollhouse:
Presage her growing ways.

She grows up so fast,
As thunder's flash of light.
She moves away to cast
An existence: her own right.
She calls home one day
Says "Mommy, I've found him;
He wants to meet you, daddy,
And little brother Jim."

We meet and we banter,
When we hear her say,
"Dear Mommy, dear Daddy,
Will you give me away?"

Our eyes filled with tears,
Our hearts full of joy,
Our heads very clear,
That rite we employ.

We wish them well,
And say we'll be there,
To assist and support
From year unto year.

They'll travel some distance.
By air, land, and sea.
Yet where'er their presence
They'll be part of me.

PERSONALITY

Too often we are so afraid,
What tomorrow will bring;
Too often we retreat to the shade,
Not let the sunlight in.

Too often we stay in the dark,
Shut out the morning sun;
Too often we display a spark;
Wilt that before day is done.

Too often we hesitate to say,
What's true and what is right;
Too often we keep prowess at bay,
Refuse to stand and fight.

Too often the world goes by.
Abdicating our slated role,
Too often we give up and die,
Bereft of an attainable goal.

Too often we blame the trim,
Not cozy enough to parlay;
Too often our errors or whim,
Constrain us to doleful dismay.

Too often we sit and mope,
Content with satiety of fate.
Too often we despair, not hope;
Not getting out the gate.

Too often we let others do,
Gain the acclaim and renown.
Too often we demurely eschew
Triumph that endorses a frown.

Too often we stray with the wolves,
Mired in the desert and dunes.
Too often we forget our loves,
Harbinger of falls and ruins.

Too often we've chosen to run,
Elected to abandon the fort.
Too often a task well done,
Not defines our mettle or mirth.

Too often we let emotions,
Distill only vitriol and hate.
Too often negate devotions,
Conventions traduce and abate.

Too often our peers we despise,
No good reason to boot.
Too often we defer to arise,
Undo a fertile pursuit.

Too often we come to regret,
Not failure, not detriment, not pays.
Too often the challenges not met,
Bestride like colossus our days.

REALITY

There are times you'll not be your best;
There are times you'll fail the test.
There are times when you need to rest,
To nurture and protect the brood in the nest.

There are times you'll not reach high;
There are times you'll be content with a sigh.
There are times you must even cry,
To let the cares and frustrations go by.

The road of life is never straight;
Some lanes are crooked, some portals, no gates.
But you must press on, each challenge negate,
For how you adapt determines your fate.

RESOLUTION

Resolve to love your neighbour,
Embrace your enemies too.
Does not take any labour
Truly not very hard to do.

Greet each morning's sunrise
Whether visible or not.
Your smile (no display of malice),
Most enduring treatise you've got.

Pass each day by, knowing
Tomorrow assured is not.
Postponing love and caring
Stains life an indelible blot.

Aver; when months, the year has flown;
Abut January and December again.
Your record, what you've done
Stands unassailable in the realm.

BEYOND TODAY

That I love you, and you love me
Is a story that will be forever told,
When decades and centuries are gone;
When today's pennies are converted to gold.

Choirs and choruses will sing,
Cymbals, ivory, wind, and strings,
Plebeians, patricians, queens, and kings,
Will venerate with wit and dispassionate calm.

They'll say we fought without lingering blows,
They'll read levity in our most trenchant words,
They'll crave our triumphs, notably when there are lows,
They'll marvel at the utterances of our crossed swords.

There is little that will not be got
From reconstruing the humanity we shared:
Content to love each other from this day to our last,
Oblivious of negations, expectations, culture, and caste.

ECSTASY

I was standing on the threshold,
I saw you come by.
I recalled our last meeting,
Then calmly put out a sigh.

The surf was so still,
So beautiful the sky.
The hour was so serene,
That star in the east would not die.

I marveled as you rumbled,
Clear sounds that excite the soul.
I whispered, perhaps mumbled,
Such charm, such grace, such elegant roll.

Yesterday you were here.
Tomorrow, next week, and next year,
You'll open your doors and invite me,
To sit, to relax, to be free.

You will hold me to your bosom,
In consummate comfort along.
You'll thrill me with your whistles,
Your puffs, tour de force, and your gong.

We'll come to the end of each journey,
You'll unclasp your arms as we are done.
We'll leave with mutual expectation,
Again together before long.

CHANCE MEETING

Your posture's so regal,
Your eyes such gleams in view;
Each moment's cast in reposal
Thinking only of you.

You caught my glance and smiled,
Your lips a natural hue;
You gaze at me; I am beguiled,
Thinking only of you.

You pause awhile, and take my hand, Your touch so warm and true,
The seconds pass, and there I stand
Thinking only of you.

You say my name so sweetly,
Your voice an endearing coo;
Entranced, impelled completely,
Thinking only of you.

You say adieu and off you go,
Never again to meet we two.
Time trundles on, my juices flow,
Thinking only of you.

The morn departs, the twilight falls,
Constraining what I now can do;
Yet I shall be, until the final call,
Thinking only of you.

PORTRAIT

You are so charming and irresistible;
You are so patently adorable.
You are so intelligent and witty;
You are so elegant and pretty.

You are indeed so creative;
You are a bundle of initiative.
You are truly so amiable;
You are palpably, conceptually able.

There are few flattering thoughts
Which may not describe your enviable path.

Who would not cherish his moments with you together?
Whether for relaxation, work, or pleasure.

Be as sweet as you are, my dear;
Like the constancy of the sunset;
Like the freshness of springtime air;
The world, your oyster will be, all year.

LEGACY

Come take my hand
Let us walk alone
Place our prints upon the sand
Our images on the stones.

We are here for a brief while,
We mark or fade away unknown.
Our work is measured mile by mile;
Shall we bequeath obscurity or renown?

We may falter on the way
We may stumble and endure pain;
As long as we get up and play,
Tasks are rewarded; goals we will attain.

We will not pass this way again;
For good or ill we disturbed the sand;
The prints, the images just lain
Inspire posterity to take their stand.

I AM FREE BECAUSE OF YOU

I am free because of you.
Your honesty, your loyalty,
your purpose release the energy that sustains me.

I am free because of you.
Your unselfishness, your caring, your understanding
support the motivation that enshrouds me.

I am free because of you.
I an enveloped by your love, parceled in your kindness;
transfigured by your prescience.

I am free because of you.
My fears dissipate, my courage inflates,
my success duplicates.

Yes! I am free because of you.
I am me because of you.

CONFESSION

Come to me my comely lass,
Rest your head upon my breast.
Caress my lips, my heart, my sash,
Repair, and be at rest.

You are a gem, a beauty,
Your eyes true love unfold.
You are inlaid with fealty,
Your touch the feel of gold.

I share no other moment,
With anyone so dear.
You clasp my cheeks and whisper,
My love, my dear, come near.

Time passes when we're together,
So fast, so fertile, so few.
No matter what the weather,
Your warmth pulsates me through.

I'll be with you forever;
With me you'll be there too.
No strife, no death, not ever
Will set apart we two.

SURPRISED

Daily he passed by and stared,
I never dreamt he cared.
One day he kissed me on the cheek;
I despised him for the better of a week.

He called to say "I love you,
I have been afraid to say.
I hope you have seen through
The emotion I did there display."

I paused at that blithe moment,
Then began to cry.
"There is no reason to repent
You may always come by."

"Hi" he said tenderly,
Those mating eyes on me he cast.
"Come and be close to me
My wish you satisfy at last."

We'll be together in glades or den,
Pledge our trust and loyalty.
Be confidant, lover, and friend,
Protect each other faithfully.

MY PLEA

Let me say I love you,
I can no longer pretend.
No matter what I say or do,
You are my morn; my day's end.

Each time I stare in your eyes,
At times you may not see,
It makes me realize
Without you I will not be.

I lay me down to sleep
You propagate my dreams;
I awake at the sound of a beep
Tears down my cheeks in streams.

Just once I felt your touch
The shock and warmth it dealt.
No one else will ever match
The way my heart you melt.

Since then when you come near,
Yet not close enough to me,
I am overcome by fear
You will never love me.

I ask that you reciprocate;
That you hold me close, and then
I will cherish such a fate;
Our lives be complete at the end.

GREATEST LOVE

Gentle, composed, and alluring,
Adorable, beautiful, and appealing.
Indefatigable, loveable, and obliging.
Lapis lazuli, lares, and penates.
That's who she is.

Buttress, buxom, and breathtaking,
Olivine, and bonafide,
That's who she is.
That oasis in my desert,
The oar in my canoe,
The rudder at the stern,
That's who she is.

Unselfish, and unwavering,
She went over there then.
Alas, she'll be here forever.
She's who I am; she's what I am;
She's what I shall ever be.

ONE MEMORY

Say, do you still want me?
Can I get you to stay?
Will my erstwhile pledged loyalty
All your fears and suspicions allay?

When we crossed the threshold
We vowed on that happy day
Our dedication and honour to uphold;
Come sickness, come sadness, come what may.

The hours now pass so uniformly,
Old passions we no longer display.
The hugs, the kisses, the gaiety,
Seem to have dissipated; just faded away.

We go to sleep at nighttime.
We drift much farther apart.
We awake to nature's new chimes;
Not one good word from us to start.

Is it truly over?
Will we vow, you and me,
To cherish the moments we spent together,
That were so pleasant, so relaxing, and so free?

MY RETURN

I have been away so long
You don't know me anymore;
I have been away so long
You don't feel my rap at the door;
Yet, I love you no less than when I left,
You are whom I cared about
Whether I stayed awake or whether I slept.

Many eons have come and gone
Our hairs have replaced their hue;
Many eons have come and gone
Memories faded as the sun kissed dew;
Yet, I prize the time spent together with you,
You are whom I dreamt about
Whether I stayed awake or whether I slept.

Our eyes meet once again
Our hearts flutter and then stall;
Our eyes meet once again
Fond memories in tearful recall;
One loves the other as when we left,
We are whom each yearned about
Whether we stayed awake or whether we slept.

SO CLOSE

You are so endearing, do not ask for much
You lay on the mat, curl on the couch.
Caress my pillow with your clutch.

You stay on my bed, on my stomach you lay
You stroke on my cheek, endear with your paws
Extend your tentacles in play.

Awake in the morning, with the dissonance of night.
You stare with precision; what utter delight!
Your coat so shiny, you're piercing eyes so bright.

I walk to the door, away I must go
You purr softly behind me, your voice very low
Assure me, the next hours will be long, and slow.

I come in the evening, put the key in the door
You are right there, your welcome you mew
There is no other; not as loving as you.

PART TWO

Humility

Hèn Oîda Oudèn Oîda:

'I know one thing that I know nothing.'

– Plato's *Apology*

THE IMMIGRANT'S JOURNEY

I am here, do I really belong?
I have come to pursue a simple mission.
Gain fame, wealth, and some recognition;
Fulfill the realization of my childhood vision.

I do not know the language, the culture, the norms;
I must compete with those who've been here as of yore;
I must make my way whether in calm or through storms,
Unaided by kith, by kin; with nothing in store.

I feel the innate suspicion of all who come
near; "He can't fit in, he is an alien"
Nervous, terrified, consumed with fear,
Convinced they've conspired to show me the den

I climb one ladder, like Sisyphus I fall;
The hours pass so slowly, the days so long and drear.
I recharge. That resilience, that force, that inner call.
I bury my frustration, keep ploughing my shear.

The years go by; success seems out of reach,
On the horizon, suddenly I sense fortune at last.
My faith is tested sorely; ere I impeach
I fall to my knees in prayer and fast.

I arrive one evening to greet at my gate,
A retinue of scribblers poised to trumpet my "luck." Will
you run for congress, the council, or the State?
The price I pay 'cause to my purpose I've stuck.

I keep on striving, relaxing some now,
Enjoying the nuances of life, whenever I can.
To assist my fellowman, I solemnly vow
To die content—life's gone according to plan.

MY FRIEND

To my friend I must say no
He wishes that I with him will go.
I have a duty to him to be true;
I cannot condone what he wants to do.

'Cause he is my friend, more to him I owe,
To assist him on the straight way to go. If I
say "yes," when I should say "no,"
I am a traitor, not a friend-worse than a foe.

TRUTH AND CONSEQUENCES

You say you know me well;
Then always tell me the truth.
I will be no greater foe,
I will be no less a friend,
When you tell me the truth.

You say you know me well;
Then never tell me a lie.
I will be no better friend,
I will be no less a foe,
When you tell me a lie.

You say you know me well;
Expect from me the truth.
I am a dastardly foe,
I am a treacherous friend,
When I tell you a lie.

The day never seems to end,
When tall tales we must amend;
The damaged image we must repair.
Lies are ephemeral; truths are eternal.
The one embalms disgust,
The other enshrines our trust.

A MILITARY SOLILOQUY

I see your echo, though you are far away;
I hear your lips, as to me they say;
Come home here with me to stay,
There'll be no greater moment, night or day.

I cast your footsteps, as you walk to pray;
I feel your pleas, as on the pew they lay;
Keep him well and protected all the way;
Bring him home safely, night or day.

I read your whisper, as your faith you assay;
I touch your murmur, as your fears you relay;
Give me the courage my distress to allay;
He'll be home whole and healthy, night or day.

Your eyelids tap as softly, as June greets
May; Your ears kiss the pillow, as your dreams you survey;
You awake at that instant, when dawn gives way;
I am home. I'll be with you every night, every day.

SUCCESS

When I can't is not an option;
When I will is not in question.
When each sunset is a sunrise;
When each scolding is an advice.

When dissent is not negation;
When an assent is not adulation.
When the debris is not putrefaction;
When inertia is a call to action.

When a loss does not portend demise;
When a gain does not really surprise.
When the dusk is not the dark;
When the dawn conjures a spark.

When to rest, but then to dream;
When to play, but dare to deem.
When to live, and yet admire;
When to die, and still inspire.

Indeed, there's no need to shout;
Prevailed you have, there is no doubt.

CONQUER

Ask, the answer will be no
Sow, the plants they will not grow.
Swim, just go under and drown,
Laugh, and be considered a clown.

Fly, the 'craft will tumble from the sky;
Vie, no one will look me in the eye.
Try, that venture's sure to fail,
Love, an invite to pain and travail.

Read, that's only for the nerds,
Sing, melody's only by the birds;
Dance, so step on other's feet,
Sail, the winds will trigger a retreat.

No for this, for that, not,
Denying the talent you've got,
Even unprepared to die,
So timid, afraid, and shy.

Begin to say I will
There are a few seconds still.
Excise the negativity and then
Inspire with your voice and pen.

Determine, the traits of brave souls
Motivate, and be extolled.
Create, your talents now extend,
Overcome, be a leader of men.

SLEEP

Quartered at the vortex of the orb's environs,
Strafed similarly by sunlight and rain
She flutters in the wind.
Her vespers summon the twilight;
The windblown petals fall expectantly
On the carpel below.

She arrests the contortions of purpose,
Of consciousness, and of design.
The paralysis of motion proximates, and
She makes her call.

It is the cusp of memory; the arc of forgetfulness;
A wade, incalculably, to that place
Where illusions beckon; a peaceful respite awaits.
A state where no one lingers;
Where everyone subsumes.
A solace serenaded by time and space;
Transcended by none; venerated by all.

WORDS

The careless words you have spoken,
The ersatz vows you have broken, Not
one scintilla of it you can recall.
The pain you have inflicted,
The tears you have elicited,
Sear the psyche on which they fall.

You may say you are sorry,
You may fall to your knees and implore;
You may try to appease with a story;
Naught will displace the discomfort and gore.

You may pray, fast, and petition,
You may repent, lament, and forswear;
No penitence, regret, nor contrition,
Will restore the faith, confidence, and care.

You may be forgiven; a neighbourly decision;
You may be regaled with The Sermon on the Mount;
Perverse, contrary, with some derision,
Words, acts, omissions; some will relentlessly recount.

INESTIMABLE

How easy it is to say "I am sorry"
Instead of being in such unnecessary hurry;
How rewarding it is to say "Please"
Which puts the listener at consummate ease;
How gratifying it is to say "Thank you"
Two little words; Ah how much good they do!

When you sit in a dentist's chair,
The anaesthesia numbs the pain you bear.
These phrases here and there
Bring peace to him who declares,
So much comfort to each who hears.
Indeed, we'll all have better days
If we remember these little words to say.

PERSPECTIVE

There is only one life we each can live;
This may be long or short.
Time and space not tagged in hours days nor years.
Seconds and minutes used to allay
Another's fears.

The memories we create,
The lives to whom we relate,
The words that endear us to our peers,
Not crave renown, rewards, nor cheers.

So is determined our lives,
Whether it is long or short,
This, the only one life we each can live.

THE EFFECT

Unanswered prayers lure one to envision stealing and to cheat;
Unanswered prayers steer one to contemplate sleeping
on the streets.

Unanswered prayers seem to deny one drink and meat;
Unanswered prayers invite one to curse and censure the elite.

Unanswered prayers present the day as being very long;
Unanswered prayers remove the melody from a song,
Unanswered prayers one's sorrows e'er prolong;
Unanswered prayers display a curve as oblong.

Unanswered prayers weaken one at the knees;
Unanswered prayers reduce the blossoms on the trees.
Unanswered prayers dim hope of the free;
Unanswered prayers invoke distrust between you and me.

Unanswered prayers preempt the respite of the grave;
Unanswered prayers cast the future as naïve.
Unanswered prayers weaken the resolve of the brave;
Unanswered prayers slim the ability, threats off to stave.

Persist! Beseech! Whatever your state;
ONE objectively scores your fate.
Your trials, tribulations, difficulties of late,
Are soon deleted, reversed by HIM we call GREAT.

One nod of HIS head, a wink of HIS eye,
All negative forces their powers defy.
Rest assured skeptic, atheist, those who deify,
Your posture, regardless, HE'll always be nigh.

THE TRUE SLF

There is a view beyond the mountain
We cannot see from here;
We must unshade our shrouded curtains,
And place our focus there.

There is a picture in the mirror
That we never choose to see;
We must unmask our stubborn egos,
And admit "that's really me."

There is a shadow that trails beside us;
That tells us who we truly are.
We must gaze on its distensions;
Consciously cede our preferred view.

Unless we make these changes
Accept we are frail and weak,
Our lives will tell a story;
Uneventful, distorted, and bleak.

CONSOLATION

There is not much I can say today,
Perchance, I am saying all by not saying much.
I'll reserve this moment so you may,
Reconcile your thoughts so your soul they'll touch.

Today will pass, tomorrow will come;
We've been some place we have never yet been.
The beauty of life is that we continue on,
Even if the road we end is not the one we began.

When day is done, the night will fall;
Yet, the sun will be there for us all.
We may be secure in knowing one thing;
A new day will dawn, and sunlight it'll bring.

FAITH

Sometimes time passes,
You think you haven't done enough;
Sometimes life's challenges
Leave you squarely in the rough.

Sometimes you try as hard as you can,
You seem to fail at everything at hand.
Take heart, friend, foe, or clan
He will sustain thee, each, and everyone.

The moonlight summons the twilight hours,
The sunlight welcomes the dew-fed flowers.
Divergent in their purpose, their path, their plan,
Each kisses the morn; mirrors the life of man.

We go to sleep, we awake; anon
We can never tell when our day is done.
Take heart, clan, foe, or friend,
He will be there at life's very end.

FIRST TIME

The leaves are green, the pasture is verdant,
The stream gleams pristinely below.
We lay on the banks with our arms together,
Distant from our childhood woes.

We draw closer; our cheeks touch each other,
We each whisper, "I love you, do you know?"
"For you my dear," came the answer,
"You are my all; my treasure; the ripple on my shoal."

We stare; our eyes in a tautless tether,
There's trembling in each of our souls.
We pull on each other, oh! So tightly,
We become one: a reed on this grassy knoll.

We kiss: so passionate; so tender, so enamored;
Our bodies folded; an accordion not yet employed.
We deepen, we engage, an experience so fulfilling,
An excrescence alluring to the other now deployed.

A scream, sheer ecstasy, pure joy,
A descant 'til we are no longer old.
Perchance we kiss, hug, cavort, on many shores,
No moment e'er to follow, displace the tale here told.

E'GAD!

I trudge along aimlessly;
No end in sight I see.
The road is neither short nor long;
No hope, no fear; nothing bothers me.

The sun comes up, the dawn breaks free;
The plants, the flowers, in the wind wave noticeably.
The birds, the bees, other creatures heavenly;
Spectacle so elegant; it's pure ecstasy.

I go along, no thought I give;
So carefree in this world I live.
How effortlessly nature provides for me;
No need to stop and ask, Who is He?

I scale the mountains, I tame the rough seas;
In lavish and splendour, I sip exotic teas.
At the end of this journey, I discover e'gad!
I'm really, really nothing, just a piece of sod.

MY PLACE

On a mountain encased by jagged hills
Suspended in the mist of nature's morns
Shadowing the furrows created by bare feet
That tread the path to the stream below
Pristine, glistening in the rays of the sun
That falls softly on the wind swept grass
Bathed by the gentle autumn breeze
That kiss the green blades on its virgin slopes
Perches this crate that gave me life.

A hovel, perhaps, thatched and plastered
Through which the raindrops fell on my bed
The thunder roared: the strands of light frightened me.
That is my place.

I share a castle now, paneled walls and roofed canopies.
Red carpeted hallways with exotic art and lofty phrases.
Serenaded by music of the great masters,
Sayings of the revered sages.
Yet, that appendage on the hillside precariously ensconced
Will always be my place.

NOSTALGIA

The little green creature lay flat.
His fragile frame on the limb.
Disguised by its foliage. He is at rest; at peace.
I approach. No! I did not know he was there.
His hue changes; he extends his tongue.
I draw closer. He lifts his head.
He hisses; he slithers. Now he darts off.
He negotiates the leaves; the branches.
He disappears in the hedge below.
I do not see him anymore.
The little green creature.
That scale clad reptile of my youth.
Yes, I see him today as I saw him then.
Nimble and agile; harmless as the
Morning dew on the tropical grass.
Hurting no one, he protects his space;
Displays his courage; inspires me,
Oh how I wish I could see him now.
See him just once again.

SEASONS' END

Rain falls on the plains and the valleys;
The sun shines on the week and the strong.
The moon bathes the streets and the alleys;
Darkness tarries not very long.

The ear of corn grows in the springtime;
The birds chirp all summer through.
The tulips, scarlet and pristine,
Glisten in the autumn dew.

Trails wind starkly up the hillsides; Streams
shimmer resplendent on the shoals.
Leaves distend o'er the rising tides,
Presage the nascent winter knolls.

Soon the seasons pass, and thus
Plants and birds suspend their play.
Ills that we do may now define us;
The good may oft be put away.

Stay on the straight and narrow;
Be true as best you can.
As the wind sustains the sparrow,
You'll be held aloft, my man.

WHEN

When:
we smile, not to court unease, we listen, not to stir doubts,
we intone, not to undermine confidence, we
agree, not to encourage hopelessness;
We exhibit faith in the other; and transform despair into elation,
doom into destiny, death into life.
We have lived, continue to live; and Our
short lives have been long enough.

PART THREE

Morality

Come L'uom S'etterna:
The moral mind is moral forever.

'To thine own self be true, thou cans't not then be false to anyone.'

- Shakespeare's *Hamlet*

THE BELL TOLLS

In the distance not far away
Distraught, disheveled, there he stood
Cocksure there'll be another day
Forsook the offer that I could.

Astride my horse which sped away
Return and spurn him yet again
Convinced there'll never be my day
Needing respite from fret, from pain

Time is a catalyst without control
Disrespect each moment at our peril
Consider life a sprint, nay a stroll Stars
will appear, asteroids prevail

The parched earth we may not till
The oak remains the acorn true
Raindrops we pray are sometimes nil The
bee hovers, the nectar brew

We are men; not gods you see
Not script a calm; not spawn a storm
In common with the flora and flea
Reduced to fossil; crypt mere adorn

In the distance not far away
The infant sips its mother's tea
Cocksure there'll be another day
The bell tolls; for you, for me.

I HAD A DREAM LAST NIGHT

I had a dream last night
As I lay there unawares
The gods who cheered me on
I did not recognize
The demons all astride.

I had a dream last night
The past lay by my side
The good deeds I did recall
Not much I could compute
The future ominously stared.

I had a dream last night
The lessons brazenly showed
Good is not minus evil
Evil not all impure
Calm and storm earth shares.

I had a dream last night
Seared with fear, dare inferred
Awoke with no regrets
No plaudits, no conceit
Allure of another day's fight.

ON PAR WITH THE OTHER

The rain rarely falls until the skies go dark,
Many a flower has a thorn on its stalk.
Good is not good for its own sake,
Evil is beauty if its lessons we take.

We gaze at the blue yonder with enviable awe,
We abhor the thunder and lightening; so raw.
Content to applaud the one; wish the other away,
Oblivious of God's intent, His mystery at play.

Success and fame are honored and praised,
Failure and indigence maligned; oh what malaise!
Results at the end are what the world treasures;
Mirth and character are far greater measures.

Exult in this axiom, whatever you do:
This orb was created not just for the few.
Plebe, patrician, Christian, Muslim, or Jew,
You're on par with the other, every one of you.

CHRISTMAS

Cradled in a lowly manger,
Halcyon in swaddling clothes.
Represented His Father as God,
Irreverent of Pilate and Herod.
Subliming repentance of one's sins,
Triumphed over death and torment.
Making intercession for all men,
Ascended to heaven; and as planned
Sitteth at the Almighty's right hand.

HE

All men were His friends
No one ever His foe.
An enigma to the end,
Foretold, He had to go.

He came one snowy night,
Nary a place to stay.
Parents in panic and fright,
Deposited Him on the hay.

So revered and so despised,
As no one has been or will
Royal fiats sealed His demise,
Yet He remains with us still.

He created and destroyed;
Spoke upon a hill.
Tamed the sea; a life restored,
Fed a throng with nearly nil.

He departed; will come again,
The faithful, so they pray.
Assured He's the saviour of men,
Celebrate this Christmas day.

WHY WORRY?

Why worry about yesterday?
It is forever gone.
You cannot affect one iota
The good or damage it has done.

Why worry about tomorrow?
It may never come.
Why waste those precious moments
Dreaming, getting nothing done.

Today is in your grasp and power
Go! get all you can done.
Make each second worthwhile
Create while there's the sun.

SOLEMN REMINDER

When you awake in springtime
And the sun so brightly shines,
When the trees flaunt their blossoms
And the leaves their rustle chimes, It's a
solemn reminder, God's up too.

When you stroll along in summer
And the raindrops quench the soil,
When the thunder claps its lightening
And the streams their gurgles boil, It's a
solemn reminder, God's on view.

When you stare at the mountain
And the crest is bathed in flames,
When Aetnas trump their rumble
And so elegantly glow in steam,
It's a solemn reminder, God's there too.

When fall greets the winter,
Showpiece a snowflake or two,
When dawn draws dusk much closer
And the daylight hours are few,
It's a solemn reminder, God's with you.

When you go to bed again
And the cries of an owl pursue,
When the crickets chirp their forewings
And peace envelopes you,
It's a solemn reminder, God's love is true.

EPIPHANY

I fall from the mountain face.
Stranded in the ditch below,
Prostrate, in perceived disgrace,
I discount the love of His grace.

I stare at the stars above.
Sedated with disgust and pain,
Devoid of all courage and hope,
I cursed at His name in vain.

I listen as the wind whisks by;
I feel the rustle in the leaves;
Frustrated and faithless, I swear
An expletive too profane to declare.

I struggle to set myself upright;
Such effort my body disdains.
I closed my eyes, and there
A voice tapped, and called my name.

Scared and astonished, I screamed,
Leave me alone, let me die.
I do not wish anyone to be
Aware of my abject misery.

Someone cares whatever you do;
Stays with you wherever you are.
Never departs, never leaves, nor deserts, Not
today, not tomorrow, not ere.

Suddenly I felt some comfort.
My eyes now fixed on the sky.
The rays of the sun peered through.
A new day had now just come nigh.

Emboldened, my legs came t'wards me,
The muscles of my arms now respond. Soon,
I am climbing the mountain.
I've reached the apex again.

I clasp my hands and mutter,
Remember, at all times my friend,
No matter whate'er life's forlorns,
He'll be there to help you ascend.

MY PURPOSE

O my God, my father,
You are here with me today.
Whether I'm good or I'm evil
You listen while I pray.

No matter where I wander,
How far I go astray;
You always take my hand,
Lead to the right pathway.

Winter, spring, summer, or fall,
No clothes, no food, no stall;
No matter what the danger,
You shield me from them all.

To care then for my brother,
Is the least that I can do.
A small attempt to proffer,
To say that thou art true.

GIVING THANKS

Pretend to be great!
That may well be true.
It is the coveted fate
Few men will e'er eschew.

You are whom you are,
None can ever be you.
Stay near; stray far,
You will retrieve a just due.

Suffice it to be understood,
Believe it yes or no.
One will be considered good,
Astride the dare he shows.

Whate'er the parts we play,
Drops on the drought-quenched bank.
O'er our thoughts, on our knees,
Confess! Concede! We are outranked.

A ROLE

We are placed on an open stage,
No curtains distort our view.
Free to display the page,
Vistas our own; our crew.

Unshackled by time, nor prey,
Constrained by naught, but our script.
We strut our tale, and have our say;
Our entrance; our exit.

The audience cheers; nor nods one wit,
Nor ember glares in rapt applause.
The effort; that tested grit
Endows us; our cause.

We yet may never know
What quests our deed foretells.
The oracles we so bestow
Bodes well; our bequest.

MY JOURNEY

I stand at the crossroads
Not knowing where to go;
Each way is similarly inviting
To the same end the other leads.

I peer in the distance
As far as beyond the bend;
The trails are equally verdant
With thorns, thistles, and reeds.

I take the one that's easiest
As trodden as the other prescribed,
Deep gorges, steep hills, dank hazards
Lanes so narrow and as starkly wide.

I know the path is well travelled
By saints, miscreants, and oafs;
The space I traverse is unspoiled

Whosoever footprints me guide.
I come to the end of my journey.
Time fades and again re-confides
A challenge transcended or defiled
And the purpose for being is expired.

Inspirational Cues

CONTRIBUTION

I shall not pass this way again.
How then may I be remembered?
Shall I make peace, alleviate pain?
Shall I regret the chips I tendered?

Any good that I can do,
The young that I can inspire,
To chart the world a better hue,
For him to craft his own empire.

Any kindness that I can show,
The purpose that I may engender;
A plaque to grit, honesty, and valour,
Testament to a soul that loves its neighbour.

Alas, I may defer or neglect it;
Betray the cause for which I came;
No record of me shall bear much merit.
And I shall have lived my life in vain.

GILEAD'S BALM

The evening will come soon enough
The shades of night will fall
Day is done, gone the sun.

The evening will come soon enough
The future will be past
The mill is run, the yarn is spun.

The evening will come soon enough
The embers will go cold
The race is run, lost or won.

The evening will come soon enough
The tale will be told
Beneath the sod, near to God.

No more pain, no more stain, at rest.
Gilead's balm.

THE INEVITABLE

You may be born in poverty or with enormous wealth;
You may experience disability or excellent health;
Yet your days will pass all the same;
You'll be gone no matter how you play the game.

Your options are clear: whether you love or hate;
You may feed your neighbour or turn him from the gate;
You may hoard your dimes, your gold, your pieces of eight;
You'll not change by an iota your ultimate fate.

You may pray, petition, caress the pew;
You may be careful, deliberate in all you do;
Your moment will come, surely by night or by day;
Your good works, your piety, won't gain you a stay.

The friends you did cherish, the foes you did create;
Will mourn your passing, may even say you are great.
They'll sip wine and cognac, your bier then entomb;
The end of a journey begun in the womb.

TWO SOON

I recall what my mother said
Before so young she went away from me.
Be true, be honest, act virtuously.
She has always been with me-as I grew.

I recall what my sister said
Before so young she went away from me.
Have faith, be kind, share selflessly. She has
always been with me-as I grew.

BE STRONG

On a dreary morn, at the crack of dawn
I stumbled to the well-kept lawn
There on the dew fed blades
Lay a crumpled clump of paper made

I glanced, then closer to it came
On was ensconced my name
By whom. I do not know
Perhaps transcribed by wind laden snow

As crisp as the air, it seemed so neat
Betrayed the hazy mist astride my feet
A dream, a mystery, destiny bide?
An apparition; a divinely guide?

I touched with delicate dismay
Uncurled like a bud on a Spring day
It read so clearly. not least opaque
My eyes widened. Am I awake?

'I love you; He does too
He's a friend, will always do
Care for you through thick and thin
Whether you lose, when you win.'

'As the elephant, as the shrew
One so tall; one of micro-view
Shares earth's woes, earth's pleasures too
He's reserved a place for me, for you.'

Some days are long, some nights grow cold
There's so much yet untold
Be strong, let naught you back hold Be bold,
blessings' be unfold.

DEATH

Death will come soon enough.
At the break of dawn,
Nigh daylight gone,
Death will come to all of us.
In the midnight hush,
In the forenoon rush,
Death will come to each of us.
Yet we need not fear,
There are comforts we'll share,
As we go over there: No more aches,
No more stain,
Immortality's gain.
Forever be at rest,
Eternally be His guest.

FRIENDLY ADVICE

Alas, hate, envy, and gore will come your way
Anger, venge, and odium, do not inveigh.
Life's journey will each repay
Those who hate will rue the day.
Those who love will earn their stay.

CHOICE

Heaven and hell are not that far apart
Each a disposition of the feint heart
We to the one or the other belong
Cause our deeds are cursed or filled with song

Truth and falsehood are together aligned
Each a deliberate penchant of the mind
The one the virtues of mankind to glorify
The other our neighbours their solace to deny

Love and hate are communal twins
Each an emotion convoked deeply within
The one charged with respect, the other disdain
One disburses pleasure, the other concocts pain

Peace and war are competing fiends
Each an exercise our power to extend
One lures and entice, the other injures and coerce
To control others the primary purpose.

Birth and death are insufferable mates
Each of a continuum we did not create
The one for which we never asked
The other an unwelcome, inevitable task

We scale the rungs of life's lofty heights
Each a chorus of wrongs or of rights
Which we inhabit at the end of the day
Encodes the breaches we traversed on our way.

PART FOUR

Mortality

Vivamus Moriendum Est:
Let us live as we must die
Cicero, *Oedipus*

'We must let go of the life we have planned, so as to accept the one that is waiting for us.'
– Joseph Campbell

I MUST GO HOME AGAIN

I must go home again
I can't from this urge abstain
Where on razored pebbles my naked feed bled
Where beneath the sod lay my ancestors' heads.
I must go home again.

I must go home again
I can't my heritage disdain
Where my nave and grit were done
Where my sinews and fibers were spun.
I must go home again.

I must go home again
I can't forget the patter on the pane
Where I felt the shade of the sun
Where pristine blue waters run
I must go home again.

I must go home again
I can't eschew the there, the then
Where lurks the gentleness of the breeze
Where there are Pecks in the fruit draped
trees I must go home again.

I must go home again
I can't elsewhere attain
Where donkeys bray and horses neigh
Where the frogs croaked at break of day
I must go home again.

I must go home again
I can't to you explain
That land, you can never know
Unless you there up did grow
I must go home again.

I must go home again
I can't relay the indulgence of men
Where I walked down the street
Where's a smile whome'er you meet
I must go home again.

I must go home again
I can't such kindness obtain
Where whether rich or poor
Where welcome deck each nabe's door
I must go home again.

I must go home again
Where the Robin Red Breast
Shares its perch with the
Buzzard in its nest.
I must go home again.

I must go home again
No other place to me
Ever so restful can ever be
Where the pig hugs the hen
I must go home again.

I must go home again
There my bone to lie
Whene'er I do die.
Don't ever dare to cry.
I am home again.

LIFE'S THOUGHTS

We oft choose whom to love and whom to hate
There are certain morsels not for our plate
Whether we smile or when we cry
Reflects the lair along we've come by.

We occupy mansions or be satisfied with less
We rise to occasions or make an egress
Musings subsumed; we thoughtlessly display
Mirrors the foal at the start on our way.

Summer rays strafe the grass until it dies
Darkness spawns the dew; aids the flora to rise
Infectious insects lurk at the revered beach
Healing properties imbed the despised leach.

Despite the this, that, where, why, what
See in each the beauteous spot
Others have the inviolate right to be
Contrary, sans; blasphemy by you, by me.

MOTHER

'Tis by the miracle of birth
Known only by a mother
That we see the first light of day
From which all else emanates.
None has near an impact
On humankind; on the world.
None ever can; none ever will;
And none ever should.

MY CHOICE

Each second as I go along
I must determine right and wrong
There are constraints I must weigh
By the end of each my day

I may dare to take the path
That now engross my heart
To thus defer may be bad advice
Delay may be a fateful choice

To think clearly and excise favour
May not be an easy endeavour
What if I conclude today
Rues my each ensuing day?

Time is short, none can deny
Light saunters across the sky
I may confirm what I may
My comfort only at play

Perchance, as I go along
I determine right or wrong
What now engross my heart
Enshrines true reasoned thought.

MY PRAYER

Why? I do not know.
Whence? Should I come, or should I go?
What? Stoop low, or aim high!!
How? Clarion clepe: 'Do or die.'

Thence: To heed the bait;
Hence: To reject fear and hate.
Option: With resolve and dogged pace,
Epilogue: Bequeath, peace, elegance, and grace.

MY VALENTINE

Whether it's noon, eve, night, or dawn
Whether life's seas are rutted or serenely calm
Be it staid, indecorous, or serpentine
You, my dear, will be my Valentine.

NEW YEAR'S

Just past twelve; just seconds ago, the world changed.
Yet nothing changed.
The sun still rises, night still falls; all goes on as before.
That one moment informs our minds, our souls
As nothing else; as no like moment.

All at once, it is the dawn, the dusk, the start, the end.
A suffusing threshold of our hopes, our fears.
It is that; and more.
It is the roar of thunder, a flash of lightning
That brightens the horizons;
Jolts our senses to our impotence, our frailty.

It is our nadir, and our vertex.
The whole world; all humankind, screams, shouts.
Moans and applauses, all that once;
Oft in unison; a chorus.
Falls asleep, awakens.
And the world goes on as before.
For we hate no less, love no more.

And nothing! Nothing has changed.

SINCERELY

May success populate the muscles and tendons of your palms.
Blessings permeate the ligaments of your soles.

NOW

Each day passes; each moment disappears.
What we do cannot be undone.
The options we defer may never come again.
For the world moves on.
The friendships we tend usually serve us well.
The associates we negate about our nature tell.
Someday we'll rue; or exult.
Indeed, we must be ourselves.
We cannot be, nor be secure, being someone else.

INELUDIBLE

Oh! We all must die
Alas! Others weep and cry.
Ah! Few grasp the pain one bears
When it seems no one cares.
When the sun goes down; the sky goes dark,
No breast, no shoulder, on which to park.

Life is a highway, strewn with woes,
Oft, this pathway sears our souls.
We trip, we fall, we butt our toes;
We end here? There? Where? Who knows?
Whate'er the *cul*, the fork, the knolls,
Fate constrains us; No this? No that? No what?
That's life's dicta. Escape, we cannot.

ON THE ROAD

If you are a cockeyed optimist,
you'll consort with potholes which will swallow you whole;
if you are a delirious pessimist,
you'll eschew the signposts that chart your desired goals.

SACRIFICE

On this Memorial Day Weekend, may I suggest we ponder that if we live long enough, work hard enough, and are lucky enough, we may own a Rolls Royce, a mansion, a yacht; yet that is all material, and ephemeral; as we will surely pass: by war, pestilence, famine, or some inexorable other.

What we say. or do, the little good thoughts and deeds, will be empyreal, and eternal.

When we strive for good; be an advocate for justice; fight for peace; It is what our friends, and foes, will long remember.

And such exercise, continually refreshes our souls.

ON THIS THANKSGIVING DAY

We eat, gossip, frolic, and play
Perchance, the Glochids on the prickly pear
Ensconce our appreciation of being here?

PASSING

The old year descends beyond the western horizon,
The new summons us from the eastern clouds,
Our hopes, our fears are extant.

We compare, we reminisce, we plan,
We project, we even make resolutions.
Yet we never know, we never can.

Fate determines our lot.
The Deity whom we recognize only by Faith
Holds considerably what happens tomorrow.

We conjure the best
Discredit the worst
That has been our year, our lives.
What then is new?

A REASON

The trees, by their foliage,
Herald Winter's Call.
The evenings earlier darken;
The snowflakes fall.
There is a reason
He does this all.

THIS DAY

This is a new day,
The bright, sunny dawn of spring;
The birds chirp cheerily,
The squirrels from the tree limbs swing;
The buds burst forth, the flowers bloom;
And you and I, in awe, look on.

We know not what will be anon;
Where, why, how, or when?
Only The Author can.

TIME PASSES

Naught we can do to change the weather
Less we can do to extend the moment.
Yet, we can relate to one another,
And appreciate each on our way;
Be aware that all is ephemeral.
Summer Falls; Winter Springs,
We are here for a short while.
Time passes.

TRUTH AND CONSEQUENCES

You say you know me well;
Then always tell me the truth.
I will be no greater foe,
I will be no less a friend,
When you tell me the truth.

You say you know me well;
Then never tell me a lie.
I will be no better friend,
I will be no less a foe,
When you tell me a lie.

You say you know me well;
Expect from me the truth.
I am a dastardly foe'
I am a treacherous friend,
When I tell you a lie.

The day never seems to end,
When tall tales we must amend.
The damaged image we must repair,
Lies are ephemeral; truths are eternal.
The one embalms disgust,
The other enshrines our trust.

YOUR TASK

It oft to me occur,
From which you may demur
Mighty Julius and a lowly slave
Is interred in a like grave.

It matters not who you are
Pauper, vagrant, or a Tsar
There's just a life to live
That endures' what you give.

To vaunt: I'm this, I'm that
An iota of which matters not
Your time, your hour, your day
Not one moment can you sway.

You may scheme, get vastly rich
Then end up in a ditch
Oh! how thus we've seen
Of emperors, lords, and queens.

The tincture of life is not shown
By wealth, power, nor a gun
More by how the race you ran
Enhanced your fellowman.

The past is already done
The future may not come
The present is in your hand
Give it! And live on.

ABOUT THE AUTHOR

The identity of the author of this book is being withheld. It is with the wish that you will read the poems without being affected by the notoriety of who wrote them. In that way, you are likely to be more objective in your praise or criticism.

Yet this much may be revealed. The author is an immigrant to the United States and wrote these poems, inspired by the conversations, banter, and discussions with New Yorkers, including children in their strollers. Most of them are, for the most part, unedited. The decision to publish results from the response of readers the internet site on which some all of them were first introduced. It is hoped that you are as impressed as the readers on that site were.

And then some other work may follow, probably a dossier of the fruits and animals of the country of the author's birth; probably a children's playbook. And I pray that you recommend this to your friends.

The author thanks you; and wishes you well.

EX_TURPI

www.ingramcontent.com/pod-product-compliance
Lightning Source LLC
LaVergne TN
LVHW040156080526
838202LV00042B/3192